International Cooking Collection

Casseroles

International
Cooking Collection

Casseroles

Mary Cadogan

CONTENTS

Published exclusively for Cupress (Canada) Ltd
20 Torbay Road, Markham, Ontario L3R 1G6 Canada
by Woodhead-Faulkner (Publishers) Ltd, Simon & Schuster International Group

This edition first published 1988
© Woodhead-Faulkner (Publishers) Ltd 1988
All rights reserved
ISBN 0-920691-82-X
Printed and bound in Italy

INTRODUCTION

Look in this book and you will find colorful and appetizing recipes, ranging from rich winter stews flavored with aromatic herbs and cooked in wine or good stock, to light vegetable mixtures laced with garlic, tomatoes or yoghurt. There are plenty of ideas, too, for the most special meal. Try Chinese Braised Lamb—gently cooked in ginger, soy sauce and cinnamon. In common with most of the recipes, it is simple to make and can be prepared well ahead of serving. Casseroles are never happier than when they are left to simmer slowly undisturbed, and need only some crusty bread or a simple vegetable to make the meal complete.

Every country has its own particular style. Locro is a favorite dish from South America where garbanzo beans and corn are abundant and cheap. Cooked with beef in a rich tomato sauce it makes a satisfying meal. Osso Bucco is a favorite Italian stew made with knuckle of veal cooked in wine. A dusting of lemon rind and parsley gives it a beautifully fresh flavor. Saffron Seafood Casserole has a taste of France and a wonderful aroma.

The vegetarian chapter proves that meat is not needed to produce a hearty stew. Sauces enriched with plenty of vegetables, with a base of good stock, transform simple ingredients into delicious dishes. Spices, too, play an important role and add their warm fragrance to many meatless meals. Dhal Sambar is a gutsy combination of lentils, eggplant and tomatoes, well spiced with chilies and cilantro leaves. For a more subtle taste, try Spinach and Zucchini Tian. If you are not a vegetarian, but in common with many of us are cutting down on meat to make your meals healthier, you will find many recipes that appeal to you.

Whatever your tastes, I have provided plenty of ideas for enjoyable meals for family, friends and special guests.

NOTES

All spoon measurements are level.

Ovens should be preheated to the temperature specified.

Basic stock recipes are marked with an asterisk and given in the reference section (pages 78–9).

Freshly ground black pepper is intended where pepper is listed.

Fresh herbs are used unless otherwise stated. If unobtainable dried herbs can be substituted in cooked dishes but halve the quantities.

Where a casserole should be 'covered tightly' and its lid does not fit snugly, place a piece of foil between the dish and lid to seal.

OXTAIL CASSEROLE WITH ORANGE

Choose the thickest oxtail available for the best flavor and buy it ready cut into large pieces.

1 oxtail, weighing about
*   2 lb, cut into pieces*
¹/₄ cup all-purpose flour
1 orange
2 tablespoons butter
1 tablespoon salad oil
2 onions, sliced
4 carrots, sliced
1 small turnip, chopped

2 cups Rich Beef Stock*
bouquet garni
1 tablespoon tomato paste
¹/₄ cup port or sherry
*   (optional)*
salt and pepper to taste
2 tablespoons chopped
*   parsley to garnish*

Serves 4
Preparation time:
35 minutes
Cooking time:
2¹/₂–3 hours
Freezing:
Recommended

Illustrated top
right: Boeuf en
Daube (page 8)

1. Trim as much fat as possible from the oxtail. Season the flour with salt and pepper and use to coat the oxtail.
2. Pare the rind from the orange, taking care not to include the white pith. Set aside 2 pieces.
3. Cut the remaining rind into fine strips and blanch in boiling water for 5 minutes. Drain and set aside for garnish.
4. Squeeze the juice from the orange and set aside.
5. Heat the butter and oil in a large pan, add the oxtail and brown over a high heat, turning frequently. Transfer to a casserole dish.
6. Add the onion, carrot and turnip to the pan and fry until lightly browned. Gradually stir in the stock, then add the 2 reserved orange rind pieces, the orange juice, bouquet garni, tomato paste, port or sherry if using, and salt and pepper. Simmer for 5 minutes, stirring, then pour over the oxtail.
7. Cover the casserole tightly and cook in a 300°F oven for 2¹/₂–3 hours, until the oxtail is tender.
8. Skim any surface fat from the casserole and discard the bouquet garni. Serve in wide soup plates, sprinkled with the reserved blanched orange strips and chopped parsley, with plenty of bread for mopping up the juices.

BOEUF EN DAUBE

A daube is similar to a pot roast in that the piece of meat is cooked in a flavored liquid—in this case a wine and tomato sauce, made more substantial with vegetables and kidney beans. A potato and carrot puree, sprinkled with chopped scallions, is a good accompaniment.

2 tablespoons salad oil	bouquet garni
2 lb top round roast	14 oz can chopped
2 onions, chopped	tomatoes
3 carrots, chopped into	1¹/₄ cups red wine
large chunks	8 oz can red kidney beans,
2 leeks, chopped into large	drained
chunks	salt and pepper to taste
2 cloves garlic, crushed	

Serves 4–6
Preparation time:
30 minutes
Cooking time:
2¹/₂ hours
Freezing:
Recommended

Illustrated on
page 7

1. Heat the oil in a flameproof casserole, add the beef and brown it all over. Remove from the pan and set aside.
2. Add the onions, carrots, leeks and garlic to the casserole and fry gently for about 5 minutes, until well coated in oil and slightly softened.
3. Add the bouquet garni, tomatoes, wine, and salt and pepper and bring to the boil. Return the meat to the pan.
4. Cover tightly and cook in a 300°F oven for 2 hours, until the meat is tender.
5. Stir in the kidney beans and return to the oven for 30 minutes.
6. To serve, remove the meat and slice it thinly. Discard the bouquet garni and any surface fat from the sauce, then serve it with the meat.

BEEF AND FENNEL POT ROAST

2¹/₂ lb top round roast	2 tablespoons salad oil
1¹/₄ cups red wine	¹/₂ teaspoon celery seeds
1 teaspoon each chopped	1 fennel
rosemary, thyme, bay	2 teaspoons Dijon mustard
and parsley	²/₃ cup Rich Beef Stock*
1 onion, chopped finely	salt and pepper to taste
2 cloves garlic, crushed	
1 tablespoon all-purpose	
flour	

1. Place the beef in a bowl, pour over the wine and add the herbs and onion. Cover and leave to marinate for at least 4 hours, or overnight, turning occasionally.

2. Remove the meat from the marinade and wipe it with paper towels; reserve the marinade. Rub the garlic over the meat and sprinkle with the flour, and salt and pepper.
3. Heat the oil in a flameproof casserole, add the beef and fry on all sides until evenly browned. Drain off excess oil. Add the reserved marinade, celery seeds and salt and pepper and bring to the boil. Cover tightly and cook in a 300°F oven for 1½ hours.
4. Remove the leaves from the fennel and set aside. Cut the fennel into 8 wedges and add to the casserole. Return to the oven for 1 hour, until the meat is tender.
5. Transfer the meat and fennel to a warmed serving dish and keep warm.
6. Strain the cooking juices into a small pan and skim the fat from the surface. Add the mustard and stock, bring to the boil, then simmer for 5 minutes. Check the seasoning and adjust if necessary.
7. Pour a little sauce over the meat and fennel and garnish with the reserved fennel leaves. Serve the remaining sauce separately. Serve with broccoli with almonds, and creamed potatoes topped with oatmeal and grated cheese, then broiled.

Serves 6–8
Preparation time:
20 minutes, plus marinating
Cooking time:
2½ hours
Freezing:
Recommended

Illustrated above:
Beef and Fennel Pot Roast

SPICED BEEF WITH BEANS

2 tablespoons salad oil	2 bay leaves
2¹/₂ lb braising steak, cubed	2 cups Rich Beef Stock*
2 onions, chopped	1 each red and yellow pepper, cored, seeded and chopped
2 cloves garlic, crushed	
1 teaspoon chili powder	1 lb can red kidney beans, drained
2 teaspoons ground cumin	
1 teaspoon chopped marjoram	1 cup Greek strained yogurt
¹/₄ cup tomato paste	salt and pepper to taste

Serves 6–8
Preparation time:
25 minutes
Cooking time:
1 hour 50 minutes
Freezing:
Recommended, at
end of stage 3

1. Heat the oil in a large pan, add the beef and fry until lightly browned. Add the onions and garlic and cook for 5 minutes. Stir in the chili, cumin and marjoram and cook for 1 minute.
2. Add the tomato paste, bay leaves, stock, and salt and pepper, bring to the boil, then cover and simmer for 1¹/₂ hours, until the beef is tender.
3. Stir in the peppers and beans and cook for 15 minutes.
4. Gradually stir in the yogurt and simmer for 5 minutes. Discard the bay leaves. Serve with rice mixed with grains.

BEEF IN GUINNESS WITH MUSTARD SEED DUMPLINGS

You will need a wide casserole dish which will hold all the dumplings, or cook the stew in two pots.

2 tablespoons salad oil	2 teaspoons Worcestershire sauce
2¹/₂ lb stewing beef, cubed	
2 onions, sliced thinly	1 tablespoon tomato paste
3 celery sticks, chopped	salt and pepper to taste
3 carrots, sliced	FOR THE DUMPLINGS:
¹/₄ cup all-purpose flour	1 cup sifted self-rising flour
2 cups Guinness	2 teaspoons mustard seeds
²/₃ cup Rich Beef Stock*	¹/₂ cup shredded suet
2 teaspoons light brown sugar	¹/₂ teaspoon salt
	2–3 tablespoons water
2 bay leaves	

1. Heat the oil in a large pan, add the beef and fry until browned. Transfer the meat to a large casserole dish.

2. Add the vegetables to the pan and fry for 5 minutes. Stir in the flour and cook for 1 minute. Gradually stir in the Guinness and stock, cooking until thickened.

3. Add the remaining ingredients, pour over the beef and stir well. Cover and cook in a 325°F oven for about 2 hours, until the meat is tender.

4. Meanwhile, make the dumplings. Mix together the flour, mustard seeds, suet and salt. Add enough water to mix to a soft dough. Shape into 16 balls and place on top of the casserole, cover and return to the oven for 20–25 minutes, until the dumplings are risen and light. Discard the bay leaves.

5. Serve with boiled thin-skinned potatoes in their skins, sprinkled with parsley.

Serves 6–8
Preparation time: 40 minutes
Cooking time: About 2½ hours
Freezing: Recommended, at end of stage 3

LAMB AND KIDNEY HOTPOT

1 tablespoon all-purpose flour	*1 tablespoon Worcestershire sauce*
1½ lb boneless lamb, cut into 1 inch cubes	*1 teaspoon chopped rosemary*
4 lambs' kidneys, cored and quartered	*1¼ cups Light Meat Stock**
1 tablespoon salad oil	*1½ lb potatoes in their skins, sliced*
2 onions, chopped	*1 tablespoon butter*
2 carrots, sliced	*salt and pepper to taste*
1 tablespoon tomato paste	*rosemary sprigs to garnish*

Serves 4–6
Preparation time:
35 minutes
Cooking time:
1–1¼ hours
Freezing:
Not recommended

1. Season the flour with salt and pepper and use to coat the lamb and kidneys.
2. Heat the oil in a large pan, add the onion and carrot and cook until softened. Add the lamb and kidneys and fry until browned. Stir in the tomato paste, Worcestershire sauce, rosemary, stock, and salt and pepper, and bring to the boil.
3. Arrange half of the potato over the base of a casserole dish. Place the meat mixture on top and cover with the remaining potato. Dot with the butter.
4. Cook, uncovered, in a 300°F oven for 1–1¼ hours, until the potato is browned. Serve garnished with rosemary.

MINTY LAMB WITH PINE NUTS

2 tablespoons salad oil	*½ cup chopped dried apricots*
1 large onion, chopped	*3 tablespoons chopped mint*
2 lb boneless lamb, cubed	*⅓ cup pine nuts*
2 cups Light Meat Stock*	*salt and pepper to taste*
1 tablespoon wine vinegar	*mint sprigs to garnish*
1 tablespoon honey	

Serves 6
Preparation time:
25 minutes
Cooking time:
1¼ hours
Freezing:
Recommended

1. Heat the oil in a large pan, add the onion and fry until lightly browned. Add the lamb and stir well.
2. Add the stock, vinegar, honey and apricots. Bring to the boil, then cover and simmer for 1 hour, stirring occasionally.
3. Add the mint, pine nuts, and salt and pepper and simmer for 15 minutes. Garnish with mint and serve with saffron rice.

LAMB AND ALE STEW WITH PAPRIKA BREAD

Use real ale if possible as it gives the best flavor.

1 tablespoon all-purpose flour
2 lb lamb fillet, cut into 1 inch cubes
1 tablespoon salad oil
2 onions, chopped
3 carrots, sliced
2 celery sticks, sliced
1¼ cups beer
1 teaspoon Dijon mustard
1 teaspoon Worcestershire sauce
2 teaspoons sugar
salt and pepper to taste
FOR THE TOPPING:
2 large slices white bread, crusts removed
2 tablespoons butter
1 teaspoon paprika

Serves 6
Preparation time:
20 minutes
Cooking time:
1½ hours
Freezing:
Recommended, at
end of stage 3

1. Season the flour with salt and pepper and use to coat the lamb.
2. Heat the oil in a flameproof casserole, add the onion and fry until lightly browned. Add the lamb and remaining ingredients, bring to the boil, then simmer for 5 minutes.
3. Cover the casserole tightly and cook in a 350°F oven for 1 hour.
4. Meanwhile, cut each slice of bread into 16 pieces.
5. Place the butter and paprika in a pan and heat gently until melted. Brush this mixture over one side of each piece of bread.
6. Cover the casserole with the bread, buttered side up, overlapping the pieces. Return to the oven, uncovered, for 30 minutes, until the bread topping is crisp and brown at the edges. Serve with leeks or green beans.

BOSTON BEAN POT

2½ cups navy beans, soaked overnight
2 onions, chopped
2 celery sticks, chopped
2 tablespoons Dijon mustard
2 tablespoons light brown sugar
3 tablespoons molasses
2 tablespoons wine vinegar
pinch of ground cloves
1 tablespoon tomato paste
1½ lb piece streaky pork
½ teaspoon salt (optional)

1. Drain the beans and cook in boiling water for 10 minutes. Drain, then place in a flameproof casserole with the onion and celery.

2. Mix together the mustard, sugar, molasses, vinegar, cloves and tomato paste, add to the pan and top up with water until the beans are just covered.

3. Bury the pork in the beans. Bring the mixture slowly to the boil and skim the surface. Stir the beans.

4. Cover tightly and cook in a 350°F oven for 2–2½ hours, until the beans are very tender; add a little boiling water halfway through the cooking if the mixture seems dry. Add the salt if using, and stir well.

5. To serve, remove the pork from the pot and cut into large chunks or slices, then return to the beans. Serve with whole wheat rolls.

Serves 6
Preparation time: 15 minutes, plus soaking time
Cooking time: 2–2½ hours
Freezing: Recommended

PORK MEATBALLS IN RED WINE

Make this dish the day before you need it, if you wish—it reheats well and I think the taste is even improved.

1 cup whole wheat breadcrumbs
2 onions, grated or chopped finely
2 lb ground pork
1 tablespoon mixed chopped herbs, e.g. sage, thyme, rosemary, marjoram

2 tablespoons salad oil
14 oz can tomatoes, chopped
1¼ cups red wine
½ lb mushrooms, sliced
1 teaspoon sugar
salt and pepper to taste

Serves 6–8
Preparation time: 40 minutes
Cooking time: 30 minutes
Freezing: Recommended

1. Mix together the breadcrumbs, onion, pork, herbs, and salt and pepper and shape into 24 balls with wetted hands.
2. Heat the oil in a frying pan, add the meatballs in batches and fry until evenly browned. Drain on paper towels.
3. Place the tomatoes, wine, mushrooms, sugar, and salt and pepper in a large pan and stir well to mix. Bring to the boil, add the meatballs and stir until they are all coated in the sauce. Cover and simmer for 30 minutes, until tender.
4. Serve the meatballs with green noodles or brown rice and a crisp leafy salad.

PORK WITH MUNG BEANS

Mung beans are tiny little green dried beans most often used for sprouting. They do not require soaking.

2 cups mung beans
2 bay leaves
2 onions
2 cloves
2 cups Chicken or
   Vegetable Stock*
2 carrots, sliced
2 celery sticks, sliced

2 tablespoons chopped
   celery leaves
1/4 lb mushrooms, sliced
4 pork shoulder steaks
1 teaspoon chopped
   marjoram
salt and pepper to taste

1. Place the beans in a pan with water to cover. Add the bay leaves and one onion stuck with the cloves. Bring to the boil, then cover and simmer for 40–45 minutes, until the beans are fairly tender. Drain, then discard the bay leaves and onion. Return the beans to the pan.

2. Chop the remaining onion and add to the pan with the stock, carrot, celery, celery leaves and mushrooms. Mix well and season with salt and pepper.

3. Sprinkle the pork with the marjoram and push into the beans. Bring to the boil, then cover and simmer for 35–40 minutes, until tender. Serve with whole wheat bread.

Serves 4
Preparation time:
20 minutes
Cooking time:
1 1/4–1 1/2 hours
Freezing:
Recommended

PORK AND RED CABBAGE BAKE

Red cabbage cooked with apples and wine vinegar is a delicious foil for rich pork. A crunchy potato topping completes the dish. Serve it with crusty bread.

2 tablespoons salad oil
1 lb pork shoulder or
  tenderloin, cubed
1 teaspoon cumin seeds
1 onion, chopped finely
1 1/2 lb red cabbage,
  shredded
1 cooking apple, peeled,
  cored and chopped

1 tablespoon light brown
  sugar
1 tablespoon wine vinegar
1/4 cup raisins
1/3 cup Chicken Stock*
1 1/2 lb potatoes, par-boiled
  in their skins and cubed
salt and pepper to taste

Serves 4
Preparation time:
35 minutes
Cooking time:
45–50 minutes
Freezing:
Recommended

1. Heat half of the oil in a large pan, add the pork and fry until lightly browned. Remove and set aside.
2. Add the cumin seeds and onion to the pan and fry for about 2 minutes, stirring. Add the cabbage, apple, sugar, vinegar, raisins, stock, and salt and pepper. Bring to the boil, then simmer for 3–4 minutes, until the cabbage has softened slightly.
3. Toss the potatoes in the remaining oil, and sprinkle with salt and pepper. Place half of the cabbage mixture in an ovenproof dish and spoon over the pork. Cover with the remaining cabbage, then top with the potatoes.
4. Cook in a 350°F oven for 45–50 minutes, until the topping is crisp and golden.

RABBIT WITH PRUNES AND WALNUTS

Prunes, walnuts and a dash of wine make this simple rabbit dish stylish enough to serve to guests.

1 tablespoon all-purpose
  flour
1 lb diced boneless rabbit
1 tablespoon salad oil
2 tablespoons butter
1 cup chopped bacon
1/4 lb small onions
3 celery sticks, chopped
1 bay leaf

1/4 teaspoon ground mace
12 ready-to-eat prunes
2/3 cup white wine
1 1/4 cups Chicken Stock*
1/3 cup walnut pieces
3 tablespoons whipping
  cream
salt and pepper to taste

1. Season the flour with salt and pepper and use to coat the rabbit.
2. Heat the oil and butter in a large saucepan or flame-proof casserole, add the rabbit and fry until evenly browned. Remove from the pan and set aside.
3. Add the bacon and onions to the pan and fry until lightly colored. Add the celery, bay leaf, mace, prunes, wine and stock, bring to the boil, then simmer for 5 minutes, stirring. Return the rabbit to the pan with the walnuts, and salt and pepper, cover and simmer for 35–40 minutes, until the rabbit is tender. Discard the bay leaf.
4. Transfer the rabbit, bacon, onions, prunes and walnuts to a warmed serving dish with a slotted spoon. Keep warm.
5. Boil the sauce rapidly until reduced by a third. Check the seasoning and stir in the cream. Pour over the rabbit.
6. Serve with steamed potatoes, green beans sprinkled with sesame seeds, and a mixed salad.

Serves 6
Preparation time:
20 minutes
Cooking time:
35–40 minutes
Freezing:
Recommended

CHICKEN STOVIES WITH PARSLEY

Always use large baking potatoes for this dish as thin-skinned ones do not cook well this way.

1 tablespoon salad oil	*¹/₄ lb mushrooms, sliced*
²/₃ cup chopped bacon	*3 tablespoons chopped*
2 onions, sliced	*parsley*
2 lb potatoes, sliced thinly	*1¹/₄ cups Chicken Stock**
³/₄ lb boneless chicken	*salt and pepper to taste*
breast, cubed	*parsley sprigs to garnish*

Serves 4
Preparation time:
30 minutes
Cooking time:
1 hour
Freezing:
Not recommended

1. Heat the oil in a large frying pan, add the bacon and fry until it is slightly crisp. Add the onions and fry until softened. Remove from the heat.
2. Arrange half of the sliced potato in a greased 2 quart shallow ovenproof dish and cover with the bacon and onion mixture. Arrange the chicken and mushrooms on top and sprinkle with the parsley, and salt and pepper.
3. Cover the chicken with the remaining potato. Pour over the stock and sprinkle with salt and pepper.
4. Cook, uncovered, in a 375°F oven for 1 hour, until the potatoes are cooked and the top is golden brown. Serve garnished with parsley.

CHICKEN AND TARRAGON BRAISE

1 large lemon	*4 teaspoons chopped*
1 boiling chicken with	*tarragon*
giblets, weighing 3¹/₂ lb	*1 bay leaf*
2 tablespoons butter	*1¹/₄ cups water*
1 tablespoon salad oil	*2 tablespoons whipping*
1 onion, chopped	*cream or plain yogurt*
3 carrots, chopped	*salt and pepper to taste*
2 celery sticks, chopped	*tarragon sprigs to garnish*

1. Halve the lemon, cut a few slices from each half and set aside for garnish, then squeeze the juice. Rinse the chicken giblets and set aside. Place the squeezed lemon halves inside the chicken.
2. Heat the butter and oil in a saucepan or flameproof casserole large enough to hold the chicken snugly. Add the chicken and fry for about 10 minutes, until evenly browned all over. Remove and set aside.

3. Add the vegetables to the pan and fry for 5 minutes. Add the giblets, lemon juice, half of the tarragon, bay leaf, water, and salt and pepper. Bring to the boil, return the chicken to the pan, cover and simmer for 1¼–1½ hours.

4. Remove the chicken, place on a warmed serving dish and keep warm. Discard the giblets and bay leaf.

5. Puree the vegetable mixture in a food processor or blender; add a little stock or milk if the sauce is too thick. Return to the pan and stir in the cream or yogurt and reserved tarragon. Reheat gently and check the seasoning.

6. Carve the chicken and garnish with the reserved lemon slices and tarragon, and serve with the sauce. Serve green beans, cooked with tomatoes and garlic, and sauteed potatoes as accompaniments.

Serves 4–5
Preparation time:
40 minutes
Cooking time:
1½–1¾ hours
Freezing:
Not recommended

CHICKEN AND CORN CASSEROLE

1 tablespoon paprika	*2 teaspoons prepared*
1 tablespoon all-purpose	*mustard*
flour	*1 tablespoon light brown*
4 chicken portions, halved	*sugar*
2 tablespoons salad oil	*2 tablespoons wine*
1 onion, chopped	*vinegar*
14 oz can tomatoes,	*1 red pepper, cored, seeded*
chopped	*and cut into strips*
2 teaspoons Worcestershire	*1¹/₂ cups frozen whole*
sauce	*kernel corn*
	salt and pepper to taste

Serves 4
Preparation time:
25 minutes
Cooking time:
35–40 minutes
Freezing:
Recommended

1. Mix together the paprika, flour, and salt and pepper and use to coat the chicken pieces.
2. Heat the oil in a saucepan, add half of the chicken pieces and fry until browned; remove. Fry the remaining pieces; remove. Drain off most of the oil.
3. Add the onion to the pan and fry until softened. Add the tomatoes, Worcestershire sauce, mustard, sugar and vinegar and bring to the boil, stirring constantly.
4. Return the chicken to the pan, cover and simmer for 35–40 minutes, until tender. Add the red pepper and corn after 20 minutes.
5. Serve with baked potatoes.

FRANKFURTER AND BACON CASSEROLE

¹/₄ lb sliced bacon, halved	*²/₃ cup Rich Vegetable*
1 tablespoon salad oil	*Stock**
1 onion, chopped	*2 teaspoons cornstarch*
1 each red and green	*blended with ²/₃ cup*
pepper, cored, seeded	*milk*
and chopped	*1 cup frozen whole kernel*
6 frankfurters, sliced	*corn*
	salt and pepper to taste

Serves 4
Preparation time:
25 minutes
Cooking time:
25–30 minutes
Freezing:
Not recommended

1. Stretch the bacon pieces on a board with the back of a knife, then roll up tightly.
2. Heat the oil in a saucepan, add the bacon rolls and fry quickly until lightly browned. Remove and set aside. Add the onion and pepper to the pan and fry for 5 minutes.
3. Add the frankfurters, bacon rolls and stock, bring to the boil, then cover and simmer for 15–20 minutes.
4. Stir in the blended cornstarch and corn and simmer for 10 minutes. Check seasoning. Serve with brown rice.

NAVY BEAN STEW

$1^{1}/_{3}$ cups navy beans,
   soaked overnight
4 cups water
1 lb piece bacon, cubed
2 onions, chopped
$^{1}/_{2}$ lb carrots, cut into large
   pieces
4 celery sticks, cut into
   large pieces
2 cloves garlic, crushed
2 medium-size tomatoes,
   skinned and chopped

2 bay leaves
3 thyme sprigs
snipped chives to garnish
FOR THE DUMPLINGS:
1 cup sifted self-rising flour
1 tablespoon snipped
   chives
1 teaspoon salt
1 clove garlic, crushed
$^{1}/_{3}$ cup suet
4–5 tablespoons water
pepper to taste

Serves 4–6
Preparation time:
25 minutes, plus
soaking time
Cooking time:
$1^{1}/_{2}$–$1^{3}/_{4}$ hours
Freezing:
Not recommended

1. Drain the beans and cook in boiling water for 10 minutes, then drain and place in a large saucepan with the remaining ingredients. Bring slowly to the boil, skimming the surface, then cover and simmer for 1–$1^{1}/_{4}$ hours, until the bacon is tender, skimming occasionally.
2. Meanwhile, make the dumplings. Mix together the flour, chives, salt, garlic, suet and pepper. Add the water, mix to a soft dough and knead briefly. Using lightly floured hands, shape the mixture into 8 balls.
3. Drop the dumplings into the stew, cover tightly and simmer for 25 minutes, until they are light and puffy.
4. Serve in soup plates, sprinkled with snipped chives.

SAUSAGE AND POTATO CASSEROLE

This is a great favorite in our family and it couldn't be easier. Hot American or spicy Italian sausages have the best flavor.

2 tablespoons salad oil
2 large onions, sliced thinly
2 lb spicy sausages, skinned
   and quartered
3 lb potatoes, sliced thinly

2 cups Rich Vegetable
   Stock*
$1^{1}/_{2}$ cups grated sharp
   Cheddar cheese
$^{1}/_{4}$ cup chopped parsley
salt and pepper to taste

1. Heat the oil in a large pan, add the onion and fry gently until lightly browned.
2. Increase the heat, add the sausages and brown quickly. Remove from the heat.
3. Place half of the potatoes in a large buttered gratin dish,

sprinkling each layer with salt and pepper. Cover with the sausage mixture, then top with the remaining potatoes, seasoning each layer. Pour in the stock.

4. Cook, uncovered, in a 375°F oven for 1 hour, until the potatoes are tender.

5. Sprinkle with the cheese and parsley and return to the oven for 15 minutes. Serve with a green salad.

Serves 6–8
Preparation time:
30 minutes
Cooking time:
1¼ hours
Freezing:
Not recommended

INDIAN FISHBALL CURRY

Sweet-tasting coconut tastes remarkably good in this fish dish, in which it is combined with subtle spices. Serve the curry with saffron rice and traditional accompaniments. A tomato salad, topped with yogurt and paprika, goes well.

1½ lb cod fillet
⅔ cup each milk and water
1 cup flaked coconut
1¼ cups boiling water
1 egg, beaten
1 onion, grated
2 potatoes, boiled and mashed
2 green chilies, seeded and chopped finely

3 tablespoons salad oil
2 teaspoons each garam masala, ground coriander and cumin
1 teaspoon turmeric
3 tablespoons lemon juice
2 teaspoons tomato paste
salt to taste
mint sprigs to garnish

Serves 4
Preparation time: 40 minutes
Cooking time: About 30 minutes
Freezing: Recommended

1. Place the cod in a shallow pan and add the milk and water. Bring to the boil, then cover and simmer for 10–12 minutes, until the fish flakes easily. Drain and flake the fish, discarding the skin and any bones.
2. Place the coconut in a bowl and pour over the boiling water. Leave to infuse for 20 minutes, then strain through a sieve, pressing out as much liquid as possible, and set aside. Reserve the coconut.
3. Mix the flaked fish in a bowl with the egg, onion, potato, chilies and salt. Form into 12–14 balls.
4. Heat the oil in a large frying pan, add the fishballs and fry carefully on all sides until lightly browned, then remove with a slotted spoon and drain on paper towels.
5. Add the spices to the pan and cook for 1 minute, stirring well. Add the lemon juice, coconut liquid and tomato paste and bring to the boil. Add 1 tablespoon of the reserved coconut and a little salt and simmer for 10 minutes, stirring occasionally.
6. Add the fishballs to the sauce, cover and simmer for 10 minutes, turning after 5 minutes.
7. Broil 1 tablespoon of the reserved coconut until lightly browned. Serve the fishballs in the sauce, sprinkled with the broiled coconut and garnished with mint.

SOUTH AMERICAN BEEF POT

It's always useful to find another recipe for using ground
beef, and this one is particularly good.

1¹/₂ lb ground beef
2 beef bouillon cubes,
   crumbled
1 tablespoon all-purpose
   flour
2 lb potatoes, sliced thinly
2 cups tomato sauce
1 Spanish onion, chopped

1 large green pepper,
   cored, seeded and
   chopped
¹/₄ cup chopped parsley
3 eggs
²/₃ cup milk
salt and pepper to taste

Serves 4−6
Preparation time:
30 minutes
Cooking time:
1¹/₄ hours
Freezing:
Not recommended

1. Place the beef in a flameproof casserole or heavy-based
saucepan and heat gently, stirring, for about 15 minutes,
until the grains are separate.
2. Sprinkle over the bouillon cubes and flour and cook
for 1 minute. Remove half of the beef and set aside.
3. Cover the beef in the pan with half of the potato, then
top with half each of the tomato sauce, onion, green
pepper and parsley, seasoning each layer well with salt
and pepper. Cover with the remaining beef and repeat the
layers, reserving a little parsley and chopped pepper for
garnish.
4. Cover the pan and cook gently for 1 hour, until the
potatoes are cooked and the beef is tender.
5. Beat the eggs with the milk, and salt and pepper, pour
over the casserole, cover and cook gently for 10–15
minutes, until the egg mixture is set. Sprinkle with the
reserved parsley and pepper to serve.

RED-COOKED BEEF

Any leftover meat can be reheated in the cooking liquid
with more vegetables or noodles the next day.

2¹/₂–3 lb shin of beef, in
   one piece
1¹/₄ cups soy sauce
3 tablespoons dry sherry
5 slices fresh root ginger
2 cloves garlic, bruised
1¹/₄ cups water
2 teaspoons honey
2 pieces star anise

2 teaspoons sesame oil
   (optional)
1 cup beansprouts
1 small head Bok Choy,
   sliced thinly
1 lb spinach, shredded
shredded scallions to
   garnish

1. Tie the beef into a neat shape and place in a pan slightly bigger than the meat. Add the soy sauce, sherry, ginger, garlic, water, honey, star anise and sesame oil, if using. Bring to the boil, then cover and simmer for 2½–3 hours, until the meat is very tender; turn several times during cooking.

2. Remove the meat from the liquid and leave to cool for 10 minutes. Cut into the thinnest possible slices and keep warm. Remove the ginger, garlic and star anise from the liquid with a slotted spoon. Bring the liquid to the boil.

3. Mix together the beansprouts, Bok Choy and spinach. Plunge half of the vegetables into the pan and cook for 2 minutes. Remove with a slotted spoon and arrange on a warmed serving dish. Keep warm. Repeat with the remaining vegetables.

4. Arrange the meat on the vegetables. Pour a little of the cooking liquid over the top and sprinkle the scallions over the meat.

Serves 6–8
Preparation time: 20 minutes
Cooking time: 2½–3 hours
Freezing: Recommended at end of stage 1

CREOLE BEEF CASSEROLE

This colorful casserole from Louisiana is traditionally cooked in a hollowed-out pumpkin.

2 tablespoons salad oil
1 Spanish onion, chopped
2 cloves garlic, crushed
2 lb stewing beef, cubed
14 oz can tomatoes, chopped
2¹/₂ cups Rich Beef Stock*
2 teaspoons chopped marjoram

1 bay leaf
1 yam, sliced
1 lb pumpkin, cubed
3 potatoes, cubed
15 oz can baby corn cobs, drained
15 oz can peach halves in syrup
salt and pepper to taste
marjoram sprigs to garnish

Serves 6–8
Preparation time:
35 minutes
Cooking time:
2³/₄ hours
Freezing:
Recommended

1. Heat the oil in a large saucepan or flameproof casserole, add the onion and garlic and fry gently until softened. Add the beef and cook, stirring, until browned all over. Add the tomatoes, stock, marjoram and bay leaf. Bring to the boil, then cover and simmer for 2 hours.
2. Add the yam, pumpkin, potato and baby corn cobs. Drain the peaches and add the syrup, and salt and pepper. Simmer for 30 minutes, until the vegetables are tender.
3. Stir in the peach halves and cook for 10 minutes. Serve garnished with marjoram sprigs.

LOCRO

This dish is popular in South America.

2 tablespoons salad oil
2 large onions, sliced
1 1/2 lb stewing beef, cubed
14 oz can peeled tomatoes
2/3 cup water
2 tablespoons paprika
1/2 teaspoon ground red
  pepper

1 lb can garbanzo beans,
  drained
1/4 lb chorizo sausage,
  sliced
2/3 cup frozen whole
  kernel corn
salt to taste
1/2 cup diced Mozzarella
  cheese, to serve

1. Heat the oil in a large saucepan, add the onion and fry until softened and lightly colored. Add the meat and fry, stirring, for 5 minutes.
2. Stir in the tomatoes with their juice, water, paprika, ground red pepper and salt. Bring to the boil, then cover and simmer for 1 3/4–2 hours, until the meat is almost tender.
3. Stir in the garbanzo beans, chorizo and corn and simmer for 30 minutes.
4. Transfer to a warmed serving dish or individual soup plates and sprinkle with pieces of Mozzarella cheese.

Serves 6
Preparation time: 35 minutes
Cooking time: 2 1/4–2 1/2 hours
Freezing: Recommended, at end of stage 3

KOFTA CURRY

2 lb ground lamb or beef	2 teaspoons each ground
2 onions, 1 grated and	coriander and cumin
1 chopped	1 teaspoon turmeric
1 inch piece fresh root	1 cinnamon stick
ginger, peeled and	4 cloves
grated	2 cups water
2 cloves garlic, crushed	1 tablespoon tomato paste
2 green chilies, seeded and	²/₃ cup golden raisins
chopped finely	¹/₃ cup blanched almonds
3 tablespoons chopped	1¹/₄ cups Greek strained
cilantro leaves	yogurt
1 egg, beaten	salt and pepper to taste
2 tablespoons salad oil	

Serves 6–8
Preparation time:
30 minutes
Cooking time:
30 minutes
Freezing:
Recommended, at
end of stage 4

1. Place the meat, grated onion, ginger, garlic, chilies, chopped cilantro, egg, and salt and pepper in a bowl and mix with the hands or a fork until thoroughly combined. Shape into 40 small balls with wet hands.
2. Heat the oil in a large pan, add the meatballs in batches and fry for about 5 minutes, until evenly browned. Remove with a slotted spoon and drain well on paper towels.
3. Drain off excess oil from the pan. Add the chopped onion to the pan and fry until lightly browned. Stir in the ground coriander, cumin and turmeric. Add the cinnamon stick and cloves and cook for 1 minute. Stir in the water, tomato paste and golden raisins and bring to the boil.
4. Return the meatballs to the pan and stir well. Cover and simmer for 30 minutes, until tender. Stir in the almonds.
5. Stir in the yogurt a tablespoon at a time. Check the seasoning. Serve with turmeric flavored rice.

MIDDLE EASTERN LAMB MEATBALLS

4 slices white bread, crusts	¹/₃ cup pine nuts
removed	¹/₄ cup lemon juice
²/₃ cup seedless raisins	1¹/₄ cups water
2 lb ground lamb	2¹/₂ cups Greek strained
2 onions, grated or	yogurt
chopped finely	4 teaspoons cornstarch
2 teaspoons ground cumin	2 tablespoons chopped
1 tablespoon ground	parsley
coriander	salt and pepper to taste
2 tablespoons salad oil	

1. Soak the bread in water to cover for 5 minutes, then squeeze well and crumble into a bowl.

2. Coarsely chop the raisins. Add to the bowl with the lamb, onion, cumin, coriander, and salt and pepper. Squeeze the mixture with your fingers until evenly mixed. Shape into about 32 small meatballs with wet hands.

3. Heat the oil in a large pan and fry the meatballs in batches for about 5 minutes, until evenly browned. Drain off any excess oil from the pan.

4. Return the meatballs to the pan and add the pine nuts, lemon juice, water, and salt and pepper. Bring to the boil, then cover and simmer for 20 minutes.

5. Blend the yogurt with the cornstarch and gradually stir into the pan. Bring to a gentle simmer and cook for about 5 minutes, until heated through. Stir in the parsley.

6. Serve with rice mixed with lightly fried grated carrot and cumin seeds.

Serves 6–8
Preparation time:
40 minutes
Cooking time:
30 minutes
Freezing:
Not recommended

LAMB AND LENTIL CURRY

2 tablespoons salad oil
2 onions, sliced thinly
1 clove garlic, crushed
1 inch piece fresh root
ginger, peeled and
grated
2 teaspoons cumin seeds
1 lb boneless lamb, e.g. leg
or fillet, cubed
2 medium-size tomatoes,
skinned and chopped

1 teaspoon each ground
cumin, coriander and
turmeric
1/2 teaspoon chili powder
21/2 cups water
1 cup red lentils
2 tablespoons lemon juice
1 teaspoon garam masala
salt to taste

Serves 4
Preparation time:
30 minutes
Cooking time:
1 hour
Freezing:
Recommended, at
end of stage 3

1. Heat 1 tablespoon of the oil in a saucepan, add the onion, garlic, ginger and half of the cumin seeds and fry until the onion is softened and lightly browned. Add the lamb and cook, stirring, until well browned.
2. Add the tomatoes, cumin, coriander, turmeric, chili powder and salt and stir well. Add the water and bring to the boil, then cover and simmer for 30 minutes.
3. Add the lentils and cook for 30 minutes or until the lamb and lentils are tender.
4. Just before serving, stir in the lemon juice and garam masala. Transfer to a warmed serving dish and keep warm.
5. Heat the remaining oil in a pan, add the remaining cumin seeds and fry quickly until they start to spit. Pour over the curry. Serve with rice and curry accompaniments.

LAMB MUGLAI

If you bone the lamb yourself, allow about 1 lb of the total weight for the bone when buying the joint.

21/2–3 lb boneless lamb, cut
into 1 inch cubes
21/2 cups water
2 inch piece cinnamon
stick
2 bay leaves
8 cloves
6 cardamom pods
2 tablespoons salad oil
2 onions, chopped

1 tablespoon curry powder
2 teaspoons ground
coriander
2 teaspoons garam masala
1/2 teaspoon hot chili
powder
1/3 cup tomato paste
11/2 lb potatoes cut into
1 inch chunks
2 cups plain yogurt

1. Place the lamb in a saucepan with the water, cinnamon stick, bay leaves, cloves and cardamom pods. Bring to the boil, then cover and simmer for 30 minutes.
2. Remove the meat with a slotted spoon and set aside. Strain the liquid into a pitcher.
3. Heat the oil in a saucepan, add the onion and fry gently until softened and lightly browned.
4. Add the lamb and the strained liquid, the spices, tomato paste and potatoes. Bring to the boil, stirring well, then cover and simmer for 25–30 minutes, until the lamb is very tender and the potatoes are cooked.
5. Stir in the yogurt a tablespoon at a time, stirring well and heating after each addition; do not allow to boil.
6. Serve the muglai with saffron rice, warm pitta bread and a shredded lettuce, cucumber and onion salad.

Serves 6–8
Preparation time: 20 minutes
Cooking time: 1 hour
Freezing: Recommended, at end of stage 4

CORIANDER CURRIED CHICKEN

²/₃ cup flaked coconut
²/₃ cup boiling water
2 teaspoons turmeric
4 chicken quarters, halved
2 tablespoons salad oil
1 onion, sliced
1 tablespoon crunchy
   peanut butter
¹/₂ teaspoon fennel seeds

¹/₂ teaspoon cumin seeds
¹/₂ teaspoon ground
   coriander
¹/₂ teaspoon black pepper
2 green chilies, chopped
   finely
strip of lemon rind
1 tablespoon lemon juice
cilantro leaves to garnish

Serves 4
Preparation time:
40 minutes, plus
standing time
Cooking time:
35–40 minutes
Freezing:
Recommended

1. Soak the coconut in the boiling water for 20 minutes, then strain and set aside the liquid; discard the coconut.
2. Rub the turmeric into the chicken pieces.
3. Heat the oil in a large saucepan, add the onion and fry until lightly browned. Stir in the peanut butter, fennel and cumin seeds, ground coriander, pepper and chilies. Cook for 1 minute, then add the chicken, turning in the mixture until evenly browned.
4. Add the coconut liquid and lemon rind, bring to the boil, then cover and simmer for 35–40 minutes, until the chicken is tender. Stir in the lemon juice. Garnish with cilantro leaves and serve with rice flavored with herbs and poppadums.

KASHMIRI CHICKEN PILAFF

2 cups Basmati rice
¹/₄ cup salad oil
2 onions, chopped
2 cloves garlic, crushed
1 inch piece fresh root
   ginger, peeled and
   chopped
2 teaspoons cumin seeds
1¹/₂ lb boneless chicken
   breast, cubed
1 teaspoon saffron strands
1¹/₄ cups boiling water

6 cardamom pods, bruised
¹/₄ cup chopped mint
1 teaspoon curry powder
1 inch piece cinnamon
   stick
1 cup frozen peas
2 medium-size tomatoes,
   skinned and chopped
¹/₃ cup golden raisins
salt to taste
¹/₃ cup blanched almonds,
   toasted, to garnish

1. Rinse the rice several times in cold water, then drain and leave to dry.
2. Heat half the oil in a large heavy-based pan, add half of the onion, the garlic, ginger and cumin seeds and fry for 5 minutes.

3. Add the chicken and cook, stirring, until browned all over. Add the saffron, water, cardamom pods, mint, curry powder and cinnamon stick. Bring to the boil, then cover and simmer for 25 minutes, until the chicken is tender. Transfer to a bowl and rinse out the pan.

4. Heat the remaining oil in the pan, add remaining onion and fry until lightly colored. Stir in the rice and cook gently for 2–3 minutes, until it becomes opaque.

5. Add the chicken mixture, peas, tomatoes, golden raisins and salt. Stir gently, then shake the pan to level the ingredients. Add sufficient boiling water to come ¾ inch above the top of the rice. Cover the pan tightly and cook gently for 20–25 minutes, until the rice is tender and all the liquid is absorbed. Discard the cinnamon stick.

6. Transfer to a warmed serving dish and sprinkle with the almonds. Serve with mango chutney, poppadums, and chilled yogurt mixed with chopped cucumber.

Serves 6
Preparation time:
30 minutes
Cooking time:
1 hour
Freezing:
Not recommended

PAPRIKA BEAN CASSEROLE

1¼ cups navy beans,
  soaked overnight
3 tablespoons salad oil
1 clove garlic, crushed
3 onions, sliced
2 green peppers, cored,
  seeded and sliced

2 tablespoons paprika
1 teaspoon honey
2 × 14 oz cans tomatoes,
  chopped
2 tablespoons tomato paste
salt and pepper to taste
parsley sprigs to garnish

Serves 4
Preparation time:
30 minutes, plus
soaking time
Cooking time:
1 hour 40 minutes
Freezing:
Recommended

1. Drain and rinse the beans and place in a pan. Cover with cold water, bring to the boil and boil for 10 minutes, then cover and simmer for about 1 hour, until tender. Drain well.
2. Heat the oil in a large pan, add the garlic and onion and fry until softened and lightly browned. Add the peppers and fry for 5 minutes.
3. Add the beans and remaining ingredients, bring to the boil, then cover and simmer for 25 minutes.
4. Garnish with parsley to serve.

CASHEW NUT AND SESAME PILAFF

2 tablespoons salad oil
2 tablespoons butter
1 onion, chopped
1 red pepper, cored, seeded
  and chopped
1 cup brown rice
2 tablespoons sesame seeds
⅓ cup white wine

3 cups Rich Vegetable
  Stock*
2 teaspoons soy sauce
2 carrots, grated
2 zucchini, grated
¾ cup cashew nuts
4 scallions, chopped
salt and pepper to taste

Serves 4
Preparation time:
35 minutes
Cooking time:
45 minutes
Freezing:
Not recommended

1. Heat the oil and butter in a heavy-based pan, add the onion and fry until softened. Add the red pepper, rice and sesame seeds and stir well, until all the rice grains are coated in oil.
2. Stir in the wine, stock and soy sauce and bring to the boil, then cover and cook gently for 35 minutes, until almost all of the liquid is absorbed.
3. Stir in the remaining ingredients, cover and cook for 10 minutes, until the rice is tender. Serve hot.

CHILI BEAN POT

The pulses I have suggested here give a good color combination and have similar cooking times, so they can be cooked in the same pot.

1¼ cups red kidney beans, soaked overnight
⅔ cup each black-eyed peas and garbanzo beans, soaked overnight
2 tablespoons salad oil
2 onions, chopped
1 clove garlic, crushed
1–2 teaspoons hot chili powder
2 × 14 oz cans tomatoes, chopped
½ teaspoon caraway seeds
⅔ cup Rich Vegetable Stock*
1 green pepper, cored, seeded and chopped
¼ lb mushrooms, chopped
salt and pepper to taste
TO SERVE:
¼ cup plain yogurt
paprika

Serves 4–6
Preparation time. 20 minutes, plus soaking time
Cooking time: 1½–1¾ hours
Freezing: Recommended at end of stage 3

1. Drain and rinse the beans and place in a large pan. Cover with cold water, bring to the boil and boil hard for 10 minutes, then partly cover and simmer for about 45 minutes, until almost tender. Drain well and rinse the pan.
2. Heat the oil in the pan, add the onion and garlic and cook until softened. Add the chili powder, tomatoes, caraway seeds, stock and green pepper and bring to the boil. Add the beans and simmer for 25–30 minutes.
3. Stir in the mushrooms, and salt and pepper, and cook for 10–20 minutes, until the beans are tender.
4. Top each portion with a little yogurt and paprika.

VEGETABLE HOTPOT WITH STILTON CROUTONS

½ lb rutabaga, diced
1 parsnip, diced
¾ lb potatoes, diced
4 celery sticks, chopped
4 leeks, sliced
3 tablespoons butter or margarine
¼ cup all-purpose flour
¾ cup plain yogurt
⅓ cup walnut halves
2 teaspoons Dijon mustard
2 tablespoons chopped parsley
salt and pepper to taste
celery leaves to garnish
FOR THE CROUTONS:
3 oz Stilton or Danish Blue cheese, crumbled
2 tablespoons softened butter
3 slices whole wheat bread, toasted
paprika

1. Place the rutabaga and parsnip in a saucepan with salted water to cover. Bring to the boil, then cover and simmer for 5 minutes. Add the potatoes and celery and cook for 10 minutes, then add the leeks and cook for about 5 minutes, until all the vegetables are tender. Strain, reserving the liquid, and set aside.

2. Melt the butter or margarine in the saucepan, add the flour and cook for 1 minute. Gradually add 1¼ cups of the reserved vegetable liquid, making up with water if necessary, and cook, stirring, until thickened and smooth. Add the yogurt, walnuts, mustard, and salt and pepper and simmer for 2 minutes. Stir in the vegetables and parsley and mix well. Transfer to a 2 quart ovenproof dish and spread evenly.

3. To make the croutons, beat together the cheese and butter until smooth. Spread thickly over the bread, then cut into small cubes, about 12 from each slice.

4. Arrange the bread, cheese side up, over the vegetables, to cover them completely. Sprinkle with paprika and bake in a 400°F oven for 20 minutes, until the topping is crisp and golden. Garnish with celery leaves and serve with a mixed salad.

Serves 4
Preparation time:
45 minutes
Cooking time:
20 minutes
Freezing:
Not recommended

DHAL SAMBAR

Don't be put off by the inclusion of whole chilies in this recipe—it's not as hot as it may appear, as the lentils add a creamy taste to offset the fire!

1 cup red lentils	*2 onions, chopped*
2¹/₂ cups water	*2 cloves garlic, crushed*
1 teaspoon turmeric	*¹/₂ inch piece fresh root*
3 green chilies, halved	*ginger, peeled and*
lengthways	*chopped finely*
1 tablespoon chopped	*1 teaspoon cumin seeds*
cilantro leaves	*¹/₂ teaspoon each*
¹/₂ lb eggplant, cut into	*fenugreek and black*
strips	*mustard seeds*
8 oz can peeled tomatoes	*¹/₂ teaspoon salt*
2 tablespoons salad oil	

Serves 4
Preparation time:
20 minutes
Cooking time:
40 minutes
Freezing:
Recommended

1. Place the lentils and water in a saucepan, bring to the boil, then simmer for 10 minutes. Stir in the turmeric, chilies, cilantro, eggplant and tomatoes with their juice. Bring to the boil, then cover and simmer for 30 minutes, until the lentils are soft and pulpy.
2. Meanwhile, heat the oil in a frying pan, add the onion and fry until softened and golden brown. Add the garlic, ginger, cumin, fenugreek and mustard seeds and fry for 2 minutes.
3. Add to the lentils with the salt and stir well. Serve with spiced Basmati rice and poppadums.

MEDITERRANEAN VEGETABLE STEW

Ratatouille is traditionally made with a lot of oil. This is a lighter version which uses just a little oil and stews the vegetables in tomato sauce.

³/₄ lb eggplant, cut into	*6 basil leaves, chopped*
large cubes	*roughly*
2 tablespoons olive oil	*1 teaspoon chopped*
1 Spanish onion, chopped	*oregano*
2 cloves garlic, crushed	*3 cups thickly sliced*
1 each red, yellow and	*zucchini*
green pepper, cored,	*¹/₃ lb mushrooms*
seeded and cut into	*salt and pepper to taste*
1 inch cubes	*cheese bread to serve (see*
2 cups tomato paste	*right)*

1. Place the eggplant in a colander, sprinkle with salt, place a plate on top and leave to drain for 30 minutes. Rinse and dry with paper towels.

2. Heat the oil in a heavy-based saucepan, add the onion and garlic and fry until softened. Add the peppers and fry for 5 minutes.

3. Add the eggplant, tomato sauce, herbs, and salt and pepper, bring to the boil, then cover and simmer for 20 minutes.

4. Add the zucchini and mushrooms and cook for 25 minutes, until the vegetables are tender. Serve with hot cheese bread.

To make cheese bread: Cut a small loaf of French bread into thick slices, without cutting right through. Mix ½ cup grated sharp Cheddar cheese with ½ cup softened butter. Spread over the cut surfaces, wrap tightly in foil and bake in a 400°F oven for about 15 minutes, until the butter has melted and the bread is crisp.

Serves 4
Preparation time:
45 minutes
Cooking time:
45 minutes
Freezing:
Recommended

EGGPLANT AND CHEESE BAKE

This is a very popular dish which can be assembled several hours in advance, ready to go in the oven.

2 eggplants, sliced
1 egg, beaten
1½ cups whole wheat breadcrumbs
⅓ cup olive oil
14 oz can tomatoes, chopped
1 teaspoon chopped oregano
1 clove garlic, crushed

1 tablespoon tomato paste
1 teaspoon honey
⅔ cup red wine
6 oz Mozzarella cheese, sliced
⅔ cup grated Parmesan cheese
salt and pepper to taste
garlic bread to serve (see opposite)

Serves 4
Preparation time: 30 minutes
Cooking time: 40–45 minutes
Freezing: Not recommended

1. Coat the eggplant slices in the egg and breadcrumbs. Heat half of the oil in a large pan, add half of the eggplant slices and fry on both sides until lightly browned. Drain on paper towels. Repeat with the remaining eggplant and oil.
2. Place the tomatoes, oregano, garlic, tomato paste, honey, wine, and salt and pepper in a saucepan. Bring to the boil, stirring, then simmer for 5 minutes.
3. Arrange half of the eggplant slices in an oiled ovenproof dish and cover with half of the Mozzarella cheese. Repeat the layers. Pour over the tomato sauce and sprinkle with the Parmesan cheese.
4. Cook in a 375°F oven for 40–45 minutes, until the eggplant is tender and the topping is golden brown. Serve with garlic bread.

MINESTRONE CASSEROLE WITH PESTO

2 tablespoons olive oil
1 large onion, sliced thinly
1 eggplant, diced
4 medium-size tomatoes, skinned and chopped
1 cup small pasta shapes
⅓ cup shredded cabbage
1 lb can red kidney beans, drained
¾ cup green beans, cut into 1 inch lengths

2 small zucchini, sliced
⅔ cup Rich Vegetable Stock*
2 tablespoons pesto
salt and pepper to taste
TO SERVE:
⅔ cup grated Parmesan cheese
garlic bread (see right)

1. Heat the oil in a large pan, add the onion and fry until softened. Add the eggplant and tomatoes and cook gently for 10 minutes.

2. Meanwhile, cook the pasta shapes in boiling salted water for 5 minutes; drain well.

3. Add to the pan with the cabbage, beans, zucchini, stock, and salt and pepper. Bring back to the boil, then cover and simmer for 15–20 minutes, until the vegetables are tender.

4. Just before serving, add the pesto. Sprinkle each portion with Parmesan cheese, and serve with garlic bread.

To make garlic bread: Cut a small loaf of French bread into thick slices, without cutting right through. Mix ½ cup softened butter with 3 crushed cloves garlic. Spread over the cut surfaces, wrap tightly in foil and bake in a 400°F oven for about 15 minutes, until the butter has melted and the bread is crisp.

Serves 4
Preparation time:
30 minutes
Cooking time:
25–30 minutes
Freezing:
Recommended at
end of stage 3

LEEK AND LIMA BEAN RAGOUT

Although this is fine as a complete meal, for non-vegetarians it can also be served as a substantial accompaniment for broiled meats or sausages.

¹/₄ cup butter or margarine
1¹/₂ lb potatoes, cut into
  ¹/₂ inch thick rounds
2 cloves garlic, crushed
¹/₄ cup all-purpose flour
1¹/₄ cups Rich Vegetable
  Stock*
1 teaspoon chopped thyme

1 lb can lima beans, or 1 lb
  frozen
2 leeks, sliced thickly
1¹/₄ cups sour cream
2 tablespoons chopped
  parsley
salt and pepper to taste

Serves 4
Preparation time:
30 minutes
Cooking time:
25–30 minutes
Freezing:
Recommended

1. Melt the butter or margarine in a large heavy-based pan, add the potatoes and fry until lightly colored. Add the garlic and cook for 1 minute.
2. Add the flour and cook for 1 minute, stirring well. Gradually add the stock and cook, stirring, until thickened. Add the thyme, cover and cook for 10 minutes.
3. Add the beans, leeks, sour cream, and salt and pepper and stir well. Cover and cook for 15–20 minutes, until the vegetables are tender. Sprinkle with parsley just before serving.

CAULIFLOWER BHAJI

Cauliflower is one of my favorite vegetables in curries as it seems to absorb the delicious sauce. Use the whole cauliflower—slice the stalk thinly and chop the leaves.

3 tablespoons salad oil
1 teaspoon cumin seeds
2 onions, sliced thinly
2 cloves garlic, crushed
1 large cauliflower, broken into florets
1 lb potatoes, cubed
1/2 teaspoon ground coriander
1 teaspoon turmeric

1 red chili, sliced thinly
2/3 cup water
3/4 cup plain yogurt
2 cups frozen peas
1 tablespoon chopped cilantro leaves
2 teaspoons garam masala
salt to taste
cilantro leaves to garnish

1. Heat the oil in a large saucepan, add the cumin seeds, onions and garlic and fry until softened. Add the cauliflower and potatoes and cook, stirring, for 5 minutes.
2. Sprinkle in the ground coriander, turmeric and chili and mix well. Add the water and yogurt and bring to the boil, then partly cover and simmer for 10–15 minutes, until the vegetables are almost tender.
3. Add the remaining ingredients and cook for 5 minutes. Garnish with cilantro leaves to serve.

Serves 4
Preparation time: 35 minutes
Cooking time: 20–25 minutes
Freezing: Not recommended

SPINACH AND ZUCCHINI TIAN

This is a deliciously light dish best made in the summer with tiny sweet zucchini and young spinach leaves.

2 tablespoons butter
1 tablespoon salad oil
1 clove garlic, crushed
4 cups grated zucchini
1 lb spinach, chopped
*   roughly*

2 eggs, beaten
1¼ cups whipping cream
⅓ cup finely grated
*   Parmesan cheese*
salt, pepper and nutmeg to
*   taste*

Serves 4
Preparation time:
30 minutes
Cooking time:
35–40 minutes
Freezing:
Not recommended

1. Heat the butter and oil in a pan, add the garlic and fry for 1 minute. Add the zucchini and spinach and stir to coat in the oil. Cover and cook gently for 5 minutes, until the spinach has wilted. Transfer to a buttered ovenproof dish.
2. Beat together the eggs, cream, and salt, pepper and nutmeg and add to the dish. Sprinkle with the cheese.
3. Place the dish on a baking sheet and cook in a 350°F oven for 35–40 minutes, until the mixture has set lightly and the top is golden.
4. Serve with sesame bread and a tomato and basil salad.

BROWN RICE BIRYANI

Serve 1 or 2 Indian salads with this dish: try a mixture of yogurt, chopped cucumber and ground cumin, or chopped onion and tomato, sprinkled with lemon juice.

2 tablespoons salad oil
1 onion, chopped
½ inch piece fresh root
*   ginger, peeled and*
*   chopped finely*
1 clove garlic, crushed
½ teaspoon each cumin
*   and fenugreek seeds*
1 cup long-grain brown
*   rice*
2½ cups Rich Vegetable
*   Stock**
1 inch piece cinnamon
*   stick*
4 cloves

2 bay leaves
5 cardamom pods, bruised
½ teaspoon turmeric
½ teaspoon salt
⅔ cup plain yogurt
¾ cup cashew nuts
⅓ cup golden raisins
1 teaspoon garam masala
1¼ cups sliced mushrooms
TO SERVE:
2 hard-boiled eggs,
*   chopped*
3 tablespoons shelled
*   pistachio nuts, skinned*

1. Heat the oil in a large pan with a tightly fitting lid. Add the onion, ginger, garlic, and cumin and fenugreek seeds and fry until the onion is lightly browned.

2. Stir in the rice and cook, stirring, until coated in oil. Add the stock, cinnamon, cloves, bay leaves, cardamom pods and turmeric, bring to the boil, then add the salt. Cover and cook gently for 30 minutes, until all the liquid is absorbed; add a little more stock if it becomes too dry.

3. Stir in the yogurt, cashew nuts, golden raisins, garam masala and mushrooms, cover and cook gently for 15 minutes.

4. Turn the biryani into a warmed serving dish and sprinkle the egg and pistachio nuts over the top. Serve with poppadums and Indian salads (see left).

Serves 4
Preparation time:
25 minutes
Cooking time:
45 minutes
Freezing:
Not recommended

KITCHERI

Mung dhal are tiny split green lentils. If you are unable to buy them, use red lentils or split peas instead. This dish can be served on its own or with chopped tomatoes moistened with plain yogurt and sprinkled with paprika.

2 tablespoons salad oil
1 inch piece fresh root
    ginger, peeled and
    chopped finely
1 onion, chopped finely
1 teaspoon cumin seeds
1/2 teaspoon fenugreek
    seeds
2 cups Basmati rice
1/2 cup mung dhal
4 1/2 cups water
2 bay leaves
1 cinnamon stick

2 tablespoons chopped
    cilantro leaves
1 teaspoon saffron strands
2 green chilies (optional),
    seeded and chopped
    finely
1/4 lb green beans, cut into
    1 inch lengths
2 carrots, chopped
1/3 lb cauliflower
    (optional), broken into
    small florets
salt to taste

Serves 4
Preparation time:
25 minutes
Cooking time:
40 minutes
Freezing:
Not recommended

1. Heat the oil in a large pan with a tightly fitting lid. Add the ginger, onion, and cumin and fenugreek seeds and fry gently until the onion is lightly browned.
2. Stir in the rice and dhal and cook, stirring, until well coated in oil. Add the water, bay leaves, cinnamon, chopped cilantro, saffron, and chilies if using. Bring to the boil, then cover and simmer for 15 minutes, until the water is beginning to be absorbed.
3. Add the remaining ingredients, stir gently, then cover and cook gently for 25 minutes, or until the rice is cooked and the vegetables are just tender.

CHEESE, SPINACH AND POTATO LAYER

2 lb fresh spinach, or 1 lb
    frozen
2 tablespoons salad oil
1/3 lb mushrooms, sliced
1 teaspoon chopped
    oregano
1 lb potatoes, boiled and
    diced

1 cup curd cheese or
    farmer's cheese
2 eggs, beaten
3/4 cup grated Cheddar
    cheese
3 tablespoons grated
    Parmesan cheese
salt, pepper and nutmeg to
    taste

1. If using fresh spinach, place in a pan with just the water that clings to the leaves after washing, cover and cook for 5 minutes, until tender. Drain and chop. If using frozen spinach, heat gently in a covered pan until defrosted, then drain, pressing out as much liquid as possible.

2. Heat the oil in a pan, add the mushrooms and fry until softened. Mix with the spinach, oregano, and a little nutmeg, salt and pepper. Transfer to a buttered ovenproof dish and cover with the potatoes.

3. Beat together the remaining ingredients, season with salt and pepper, then spread over the potatoes.

4. Cook in a 350°F oven for 40 minutes, until risen and deep golden brown. Serve immediately, with a mixed salad if you wish.

Serves 4
Preparation time: 30 minutes
Cooking time: 40 minutes
Freezing: Not recommended

YAM AND CELERIAC BAKE

1 lb yams
1 lb celeriac, peeled
1¼ cups sour cream
1 cup grated Gruyère
  cheese
⅓ cup finely grated
  Parmesan cheese

1 small onion, chopped
  finely
3 scallions, chopped
¼ cup medium oatmeal
1 tablespoon butter
salt and pepper to taste

Serves 4
Preparation time:
30 minutes
Cooking time:
1 hour
Freezing:
Not recommended

1. Cut the yams and celeriac into thin slices; cut the slices into halves or quarters if large. Par-boil in salted water for 5 minutes, then drain.
2. Mix together the sour cream, cheeses, onion, scallions, and salt and pepper.
3. Place half of the yams and celeriac in a buttered ovenproof dish. Spread with half of the cream mixture. Repeat the layers. Sprinkle with the oatmeal and dot with the butter.
4. Bake in a 350°F oven for 1 hour, until the vegetables are tender and the topping is golden brown. Serve with a green salad if you wish.

WINTER NUT CRUMBLE

1 cup roughly chopped
  carrots
2 parsnips, diced
1 small rutabaga, diced
1 leek, sliced
⅔ cup milk
1¼ cups Rich Vegetable
  Stock*
1 lb can chestnuts, drained
2 tablespoons cornstarch,
  blended with
  1 tablespoon water

salt and pepper to taste
fresh herbs to garnish
FOR THE TOPPING:
3 tablespoons sunflower
  seeds
¼ cup chopped nuts
1 cup whole wheat
  breadcrumbs
½ cup grated sharp
  Cheddar

Serves 4
Preparation time:
40 minutes
Cooking time:
About 30 minutes
Freezing:
Recommended

1. Place the vegetables in a pan with the milk and stock and bring to the boil. Partly cover and simmer for 15–20 minutes, until almost tender. Add the chestnuts, and salt and pepper, and stir well.
2. Stir in the blended cornstarch and cook until thickened and smooth, stirring constantly.
3. Transfer the mixture to a warmed ovenproof dish. Mix together the topping ingredients and sprinkle evenly over

the top. Broil for 5 minutes, until the topping is crisp and golden brown. Serve immediately, garnished with fresh herbs.

MONGOLIAN HOTPOT

This dish is the Chinese version of a fondue—the morsels of food are cooked in simmering stock at the table, then dipped into various sauces. If you don't happen to have an authentic Chinese firepot, use a fondue pot, or a small burner with a flameproof casserole on top. The food is removed from the stock, using small wire baskets which are available from Chinese shops. Serve the hotpot with a bowl of boiled rice and jasmine tea.

4 lb lamb fillet
1/3 lb rice vermicelli or egg noodles
1 lb young collard greens, shredded
1 lb Bok Choy, shredded
1 cup bean sprouts
7 1/2 cups Chicken Stock*
scallion brushes (see page 69) to garnish

FOR THE DIPS:
1/3 cup soy sauce
1 tablespoon finely chopped scallion
1 teaspoon grated fresh root ginger
1/4 cup chili sauce
1/4 cup hoisin sauce

Serves 8–10
Preparation time: 45 minutes
Cooking time: Variable (depending on stock temperature, number of diners, etc)
Freezing: Not recommended

1. Using a large very sharp knife, cut the lamb into very thin slices.
2. Break up the rice vermicelli, if using, and place in a large bowl. Cover with hot water and soak for 15 minutes, until softened; drain. If using egg noodles, cook according to package instructions; drain.
3. Arrange the lamb, rice vermicelli or egg noodles, collard greens, Bok Choy and bean sprouts on several serving dishes around the table. Garnish with scallion brushes. Bring the stock to the boil.
4. Mix together the soy sauce, scallion and ginger. Place in several tiny dishes. Put the chili sauce and hoisin sauce into several more dishes. Place on the table.
5. Bring the boiling stock to the table. Everyone should have a dinner plate or Chinese bowl, a set of chopsticks and a wire basket. The basket is filled with morsels of food, then lowered into the stock until the food is cooked. The stock must be kept simmering.
6. Use the dips to accompany the food. The food imparts ever increasing flavor to the stock, which is finally drunk as a soup in small bowls at the end of the meal.

CHINESE BRAISED LAMB

This aromatic lamb dish is wonderful for a special occasion. It can be prepared up to the end of stage 2 the day before, if necessary.

2 tablespoons salad oil
1¹/₂ lb boneless lamb, e.g.
    fillet or leg, cut into
    1¹/₂ inch pieces
2 slices fresh root ginger,
    cut into thin strips
1 onion, sliced thinly
2 cups Chicken Stock*
¹/₄ cup light brown sugar,
    packed

2 tablespoons soy sauce
1 inch piece cinnamon
    stick
1 tablespoon smooth
    peanut butter
1 tablespoon hoisin sauce
8 scallions
¹/₄ lb mushrooms, sliced

Serves 4
Preparation time:
25 minutes
Cooking time:
1–1¹/₄ hours
Freezing:
Recommended at
end of stage 2

1. Heat the oil in a large pan, add the lamb and fry quickly, stirring, until browned. Add the ginger and onion and fry until softened.
2. Add the stock, sugar, soy sauce, cinnamon, peanut butter and hoisin sauce, bring to the boil, stirring, then cover and simmer for 1–1¹/₄ hours, until the lamb is tender.
3. Meanwhile, make brushes (see page 69) from 4 of the scallions; slice the remainder diagonally.
4. Five minutes before the end of the cooking time, add the sliced scallions and mushrooms to the lamb.
5. Serve garnished with the scallion brushes, and accompanied by boiled rice and blanched lettuce leaves sprinkled with oyster sauce.

PORK IN CIDER

Pork is generally a tender meat which needs less cooking than you might imagine.

¹/₄ cup all-purpose flour
2 teaspoons paprika
1 teaspoon dry mustard
1¹/₂ lb lean pork, cut into
    cubes
2 tablespoons salad oil
1 onion, sliced

2 cups apple cider
1 cooking apple, peeled,
    cored and sliced
1 small red pepper, cored,
    seeded and diced
3 tablespoons heavy cream
salt and pepper to taste

1. Mix together the flour, paprika and mustard and use to coat the pork.

2. Heat the oil in a heavy-based saucepan, add the onion and fry until softened. Add the pork and fry until browned all over. Add any leftover flour mixture and cook for 1 minute.

3. Gradually stir in the cider and cook, stirring, until thickened and smooth. Add the apple, and salt and pepper and stir well. Cover and simmer for 40 minutes, until the pork is tender; add the red pepper after 25 minutes.

4. Just before serving, stir in the cream and heat through. Serve with pasta and a green salad.

Serves 4
Preparation time: 25 minutes
Cooking time: 40 minutes
Freezing: Recommended at end of stage 3

CASSOULET ROBERT

Cassoulet originates in South West France, where every town has its own version. This recipe may not be strictly authentic, but it is a favorite in my house.

2¹/₂ cups navy beans,
*   soaked overnight*
1¹/₂ lb salt belly pork
half shoulder of lamb,
*   weighing about 1¹/₂ lb,*
*   boned*
4 leeks
4 large carrots
2 cloves
1 large onion
2 thyme sprigs

4 cloves garlic
4 medium-size ripe
*   tomatoes, skinned and*
*   quartered*
1 tablespoon salad oil
1 lb coarse spicy sausage
1 cup fresh brown
*   breadcrumbs*
salt and pepper to taste
thyme sprigs to garnish

Serves 8
Preparation time:
30 minutes, plus
soaking time
Cooking time:
4 hours
Freezing:
Recommended

1. Drain and rinse the beans and cook in boiling water for 10 minutes. Drain, then place in a very large pan with water to cover. Bury the pork and lamb in the beans.
2. Tie 2 leeks together. Halve 2 carrots lengthways. Stick the cloves into the onion. Place these vegetables in the pan with the thyme, 2 garlic cloves and plenty of black pepper.
3. Bring slowly to the boil, skimming the surface, then cover and simmer for about 1½ hours, skimming occasionally, until the beans are tender.
4. Remove the meat and strain the beans, reserving the stock. Remove the vegetables and thyme from the beans. Taste the stock and add salt if necessary.
5. Remove the rind from the pork. Cut the pork and lamb into 1 inch chunks.
6. Crush the remaining garlic and mix with the tomatoes.
7. Place half of the beans in a large casserole. Cover with the meat, then the tomatoes. Place the remaining beans on top. Pour over 2½ cups of the reserved stock and cover tightly.
8. Cook in a 275°F oven for 1½ hours; add more stock if it becomes too dry.
9. Heat the oil in a pan, add the sausage and fry until well browned. Drain and cut into 2 inch lengths. Stir into the beans. Sprinkle the breadcrumbs over the top. Return to the oven, uncovered, for 1 hour, until the top is crusty and golden brown.
10. Serve garnished with thyme, with plenty of warm French bread to mop up the juices, and a green salad.

BRAISED STUFFED PORK FILLET

1 pork fillet, weighing about 1 lb	*1 onion, chopped finely*
	1¼ cups Light Meat Stock*
⅓ cup dried apricots, soaked if necessary	*2 tablespoons lemon juice*
	¼ lb mushrooms, sliced
4–6 sage leaves	*2 tablespoons sherry*
2 tablespoons roughly chopped parsley	*⅔ cup sour cream*
	salt and pepper to taste
1 tablespoon salad oil	*sage leaves to garnish*

Serves 4
Preparation time:
30 minutes
Cooking time:
35 minutes
Freezing:
Not recommended

1. Slice the pork fillet almost in half horizontally. Open out and flatten with a rolling pin or meat mallet. Arrange the apricots and sage leaves down one half and sprinkle with the parsley, and salt and pepper. Fold the other half over the filling and secure with cocktail sticks or fine string.
2. Heat the oil in a large frying pan with a lid, add the pork and fry until browned all over. Remove from the pan and keep warm.
3. Add the onion to the pan and fry until softened. Add the stock and lemon juice and bring to the boil. Return the meat to the pan, cover and simmer for 20 minutes.
4. Stir in the mushrooms and sherry and mix well. Season with salt and pepper. Cook for 15 minutes. Remove the pork, discarding the cocktail sticks or string, and keep warm.
5. Gradually stir the sour cream into the sauce, heating gently but not allowing it to boil.
6. Slice the pork thinly and arrange on warmed individual plates. Spoon the mushroom sauce around the pork and garnish with sage leaves. Serve with boiled thin-skinned potatoes or plain boiled rice.

AFELIA

This is a typical Greek dish, using a few simple ingredients to maximum effect.

2 tablespoons coriander seeds	*2 tablespoons salad oil*
	1 onion, sliced thinly
1½ lb lean boneless pork, cubed	*2 teaspoons all-purpose flour*
1¼ cups red wine	*salt and pepper to taste*

1. Crush the coriander seeds lightly in a pestle and mortar or with the back of a wooden spoon. Place the pork in a china bowl. Add the coriander and wine, cover and marinate for at least 6 hours, or overnight if possible.

2. Remove the meat with a slotted spoon and dry with paper towels; reserve the marinade.

3. Heat the oil in a heavy-based pan, add the onion and fry until softened. Add the pork and fry until browned all over. Sprinkle in the flour and cook for 1 minute.

4. Gradually add the marinade, stirring until slightly thickened. Season with salt and pepper. Cover and simmer for 40–50 minutes, until the pork is tender.

5. Serve with tomato rice pilaff: cook the rice with 1 tablespoon tomato paste, then stir in a can of drained and halved artichoke hearts and chopped parsley to taste.

Serves 4
Preparation time: 25 minutes, plus marinating
Cooking time: 40–50 minutes
Freezing: Recommended

BEEF AND ROSEMARY ROLL-UPS

8 thin slices flank steak	*2 tablespoons salad oil*
8 slices Parma ham	*1 onion, chopped*
2 tablespoons chopped	*²/₃ cup red wine*
parsley	*²/₃ cup Rich Beef Stock**
2 teaspoons finely chopped	*2 medium-size tomatoes,*
rosemary	*skinned and chopped*
¹/₃ cup grated Parmesan	*salt and pepper to taste*
cheese	*rosemary sprigs to garnish*

Serves 4
Preparation time:
25 minutes
Cooking time:
50–60 minutes
Freezing:
Recommended

1. Sprinkle the beef slices with salt and pepper and place a slice of Parma ham on top. Mix together the parsley, rosemary and Parmesan. Place a little of the mixture on one end of each beef slice. Roll up, tucking in the ends to enclose the filling, and secure with fine string or cocktail sticks.
2. Heat the oil in a large saucepan, add the onion and fry until softened. Add the beef and fry until browned.
3. Add the wine, stock and tomatoes, bring to the boil, then cover and simmer for 50–60 minutes, until the beef is tender. Remove the string or cocktail sticks and arrange the beef on a warmed serving dish.
4. Pour over the sauce, garnish with rosemary and serve with rice cooked with chopped spinach and 1 tablespoon tomato paste.

BEEF IN RED WINE

An ideal dish for entertaining: it can be made up to two days in advance and, in fact, improves with reheating.

1¹/₂ lb chuck steak or top	*2 tablespoons salad oil*
rump, cut into large	*2 tablespoons butter*
cubes	*¹/₂ lb pearl onions*
1 onion, sliced thinly	*¹/₄ cup all-purpose flour*
6 peppercorns	*1 clove garlic, crushed*
bouquet garni	*³/₄ lb mushrooms*
2 tablespoons brandy	*salt and pepper to taste*
2 cups full-bodied red	*French bread slices, toasted,*
wine	*to garnish*
4 strips bacon, halved	

1. Place the meat in a large bowl. Sprinkle with the onion slices, then add the peppercorns, bouquet garni, brandy and wine. Stir well and leave to marinate for 3–4 hours, or

overnight, stirring occasionally. Strain, reserving the marinade, and dry the meat with paper towels.

2. Stretch the bacon with the back of a knife, then roll up, securing with a cocktail stick if necessary.

3. Heat the oil and butter in a large pan, add the bacon rolls and fry until lightly browned. Remove with a slotted spoon and set aside.

4. Add the small onions to the pan and fry until lightly browned; remove and set aside.

5. Add the beef to the pan and fry over a high heat until evenly browned. Sprinkle in the flour and cook, stirring, for 1 minute. Add the reserved marinade and bring to the boil, stirring. Add the garlic, and salt and pepper, then cover and simmer for 2 hours, until tender.

6. Remove the cocktail sticks from the bacon rolls, add to the pan with the onions and mushrooms and simmer for 30 minutes. Garnish with toasted French bread to serve.

Serves 4
Preparation time:
30 minutes, plus marinating
Cooking time:
2½ hours
Freezing:
Recommended

OSSO BUCCO WITH GREMOLATA

Shin of veal can be ordered from the meat counter.

*1 tablespoon all-purpose
flour
4 slices shin of veal, about
1¹/₂ inches thick
2 tablespoons butter
1 tablespoon olive oil
2 onions, chopped
2 carrots, chopped
1 stick celery, chopped
1¹/₄ cups dry white wine*

*8 oz can chopped tomatoes
bouquet garni
2 strips lemon rind
salt and pepper to taste
FOR THE GREMOLATA:
1 teaspoon grated lemon
rind
1 clove garlic, crushed
2 tablespoons chopped
parsley*

Serves 4
Preparation time:
30 minutes
Cooking time:
1 hour
Freezing:
Recommended

1. Season the flour with salt and pepper and use to coat the veal.
2. Heat the butter and oil in a large saucepan, add the veal and brown all over. Remove from the pan and set aside.
3. Add the onion, carrot and celery to the pan and fry for 5 minutes, until slightly softened. Add the remaining ingredients and bring to the boil. Return the veal to the pan, cover and simmer for 1 hour, until the veal is tender.
4. Mix together the gremolata ingredients. Sprinkle a little over each portion of osso bucco to serve.

BEEF ROLLS IN WATERCRESS SAUCE

*²/₃ cup finely chopped
zucchini
2 strips Canadian bacon,
chopped
2 teaspoons capers,
chopped
1 teaspoon chopped
marjoram
1 teaspoon Dijon mustard
8 thin slices flank steak*

*1 tablespoon salad oil
2 tablespoons butter
1 leek, chopped finely
²/₃ cup dry white wine
1 bunch watercress
3 tablespoons heavy cream
salt and pepper to taste
TO GARNISH:
watercress sprigs
orange slices*

1. Mix together the zucchini, bacon, capers, marjoram and mustard. Season lightly with salt and pepper. Place a little of the mixture on one end of each steak, roll up, tucking in the ends to enclose the filling, and secure with fine string or cocktail sticks.
2. Heat the oil and butter in a wide pan, add the beef rolls

and fry until lightly browned all over. Remove from the pan and set aside.

3. Add the leek to the pan and fry gently for 2 minutes. Stir in the wine and bring to the boil. Season with salt and pepper.

4. Return the beef to the pan, cover and simmer for 1 hour, until tender. Remove from the pan, remove the string or cocktail sticks and keep warm.

5. Add the watercress to the pan and cook for 1–2 minutes, until wilted but still bright green. Puree in a blender or food processor, return to the pan, stir in the cream and reheat gently.

6. Spoon a pool of sauce onto each warmed dinner plate and arrange 2 beef rolls on top. Garnish with watercress and orange and serve with tiny thin-skinned potatoes.

Serves 4
Preparation time:
35 minutes
Cooking time:
1 hour
Freezing:
Not recommended

MONKFISH AND BACON WITH WINE AND HERB SAUCE

¹/₃ lb sliced bacon, halved   *²/₃ cup dry white wine*
1¹/₂ lb monkfish, cut into   *²/₃ cup Chicken Stock**
*   2 × 1 inch pieces*   *2 teaspoons all-purpose*
1 tablespoon olive oil   *   flour*
2 shallots, chopped   *2 tablespoons butter*
1 clove garlic, crushed   *¹/₄ cup chopped parsley*
¹/₂ lb small mushrooms   *salt and pepper to taste*
*   (optional)*   *dill sprigs to garnish*
1 teaspoon chopped dill

Serves 4
Preparation time:
30 minutes
Cooking time:
25–30 minutes
Freezing:
Not recommended

1. Stretch the bacon with the back of a knife and wrap a half strip around each piece of fish.
2. Heat the oil in a saucepan, add the fish and fry gently for about 5 minutes, until the bacon is lightly browned. Remove with a slotted spoon and set aside.
3. Add the shallots and garlic to the pan and fry until softened. Add the mushrooms, if using, and dill and cook, stirring for 2 minutes. Add the wine and stock and bring to the boil.
4. Return the fish to the pan and simmer for 15–20 minutes, until tender. Season with salt and pepper.
5. Mash together the flour and butter until smooth. Add a little piece at a time to the simmering liquid, cooking until slightly thickened. Stir in the parsley. Serve garnished with dill, with a risotto of chopped tomatoes and peppers.

BLANQUETTE OF SOLE WITH CUCUMBER

Cooked cucumber may be unfamiliar to you, but it adds a fresh taste to the subtle fish and cream sauce.

8 lemon sole fillets, each   *²/₃ cup dry white wine*
*   weighing about ¹/₄ lb,*   *2 tablespoons freshly*
*   skinned*   *   squeezed orange juice*
¹/₂ cucumber, peeled   *²/₃ cup whipping cream*
2 tablespoons butter   *1 egg yolk*
1 small onion, chopped   *salt and pepper to taste*
*   finely*

1. Season the sole fillets on the skinned side with salt and pepper, then fold each into three.

2. Cut the cucumber into 1 inch slices, then cut each slice into quarters.

3. Melt the butter in a large frying pan with a lid. Add the onion and fry gently until softened. Add the cucumber and fry for 2 minutes.

4. Place the fish in the pan, pour over the wine and orange juice, bring to simmering point, then cover and cook for 7–10 minutes, until tender.

5. Transfer the fish and cucumber to a warmed serving dish with a spatula, cover and keep warm while making the sauce.

6. Strain the pan juices, return to the pan and bring to the boil. Mix together the cream and egg yolk, stir into the pan and simmer gently, stirring constantly, until thickened. Check the seasoning.

7. Pour a little sauce over each fillet and hand the rest separately. Serve with thin-skinned potatoes and a Belgium endive and orange salad.

Serves 4
Preparation time:
30 minutes
Cooking time:
About 20 minutes
Freezing:
Not recommended

SAFFRON SEAFOOD CASSEROLE

1/4 cup butter
1 clove garlic, crushed
2 onions, chopped
1 leek, sliced thinly
1 lb haddock fillet, skinned
  and cubed
1 lb small thin-skinned
  potatoes
1 1/4 cups white wine
1 1/4 cups whipping cream

1/2 teaspoon saffron
  strands
1/4 lb medium-size scallops
1/4 lb shelled mussels
1/4 lb medium-size shelled
  shrimp
1/4 lb crabmeat
1 teaspoon chopped
  tarragon
salt and pepper to taste
tarragon sprigs to garnish

Serves 4
Preparation time:
25 minutes
Cooking time:
30–35 minutes
Freezing:
Not recommended

1. Melt the butter in a large pan, add the garlic, onion and leek and cook until softened. Add the haddock and potatoes and stir well.
2. Add the wine, cream and saffron, bring to the boil, then cover and simmer for 20 minutes.
3. Stir in the remaining ingredients carefully and simmer for 10–15 minutes, until the potatoes are tender.
4. Serve garnished with tarragon, with French bread.

CHICKEN RICE

This recipe is adapted from a Malaysian dish. The chicken is steamed over the aromatic rice to make it moist and tender. I serve a fiery dipping sauce with it.

1 lb boneless chicken
  breast, cut into 1 inch
  cubes
2 tablespoons soy sauce
2 tablespoons salad oil
1 tablespoon grated fresh
  root ginger
2 cloves garlic, crushed
1 1/2 cups Basmati rice
2 1/2 cups Chicken Stock*

FOR THE DIPPING SAUCE:
1 red or green chili
2 tablespoons grated fresh
  root ginger
2 cloves garlic, crushed
2 tablespoons sesame oil
salt to taste
TO GARNISH:
scallion brushes and chili
  flowers (see right)
cucumber slices

1. Place the chicken and soy sauce in a bowl and mix well.
2. Heat the oil in a flameproof casserole, add the ginger and garlic and fry until lightly browned. Add the rice, stirring until coated in the oil.

3. Add the stock and a little salt, bring to the boil, then cover and simmer for about 5 minutes, until the rice has absorbed some of the stock.

4. Place the chicken over the rice in one layer and sprinkle with any remaining soy sauce. Cover and cook for 20–25 minutes, until the chicken and rice are tender.

5. Meanwhile, make the dipping sauce. Cut the chili in half lengthways and remove the seeds and stalk. Chop the chili very finely and mix in a small bowl with the ginger, garlic, sesame oil and a little salt.

6. Transfer the chicken rice to a warmed serving dish. Garnish with scallion brushes, chili flowers and cucumber slices. Hand the dipping sauce separately.

To make scallion brushes: Cut the scallions into 2 inch lengths. Make cross-cuts at each end of each piece, almost to the center. Place in salted ice water to open out.

To make chili flowers: Cut down the chili from near the base to the tip. Make a second cut at right angles to this. Remove the seeds. Place in ice water and the chili will open like a flower.

Serves 4
Preparation time:
25 minutes
Cooking time:
About 30 minutes
Freezing:
Not recommended

Illustrated on
page 71

HOWTOWDIE WITH DRAPPIT EGGS

This unusual sounding dish is a traditional Scottish recipe.

1 broiler-fryer chicken,
  with giblets, weighing
  4 lb
1 cup fresh breadcrumbs
¼ cup milk
1 small onion, chopped
2 teaspoons chopped
  tarragon
1 tablespoon chopped
  parsley

¼ cup butter
8 shallots
2 celery sticks, chopped
pinch of ground mace
pinch of ground cloves
2 cups Chicken Stock*
4–6 eggs
⅔ cup heavy cream
1½ lb spinach
salt and pepper to taste

Serves 4–6
Preparation time:
40 minutes
Cooking time:
About 1¼ hours
Freezing:
Not recommended

Illustrated below
right: Chicken Rice
(page 68)

1. Remove the giblets from the chicken, rinse thoroughly and set aside. Wipe the chicken and sprinkle inside and out with salt and pepper.
2. Soak the breadcrumbs in the milk for a few minutes, until softened, then mix with the onion, herbs, and salt and pepper. Use to stuff the neck end of the chicken and secure with a fine skewer.
3. Melt the butter in a flameproof casserole, add the shallots and fry until lightly browned. Remove with a slotted spoon and set aside.
4. Add the chicken to the pan and fry until browned all over. Add the shallots, celery, mace, cloves, giblets and stock, bring to the boil, then cover tightly and cook for about 1¼ hours, until the chicken is tender.
5. Transfer the chicken to a serving dish and keep warm.
6. Strain the stock into a clean pan, pressing through as much of the chicken liver as possible; skim the surface. Boil for 5 minutes, until reduced slightly, then lower the heat to simmer. Drop in the eggs and poach for 4–5 minutes, until set. Remove with a slotted spoon and keep warm in a shallow pan of warm water.
7. Meanwhile, cook the spinach in a covered pan, with no extra water, for about 5 minutes, until tender. Season with salt and pepper.
8. Stir the cream into the stock and reheat. Check the seasoning.
9. Arrange the spinach around the chicken and place the eggs on top. Pour a little sauce over the chicken and serve the remainder separately.

BRAISED CHICKEN BREASTS

*½ teaspoon dried
   rosemary*
1 clove garlic, crushed
*2 tablespoons softened
   butter*
*2 tablespoons grated
   Parmesan cheese*
*4 partly boned chicken
   breasts, each weighing
   about ⅓ lb*

3 carrots
3 celery sticks
2 leeks
1 tablespoon salad oil
2 tablespoons butter
⅔ cup Chicken Stock*
2 tablespoons lemon juice
salt and pepper to taste

Serves 4
Preparation time:
35 minutes, plus
chilling
Cooking time:
30–35 minutes
Freezing:
Recommended

1. Mix together the rosemary, garlic, butter, cheese, and salt and pepper. Loosen the skin from the chicken and spread a little mixture between the flesh and skin. Smooth the skin back over the stuffing. Chill for 30 minutes.
2. Cut the carrots, celery and leeks into matchstick pieces.
3. Heat the oil and butter in a large heavy-based casserole, add the chicken and fry quickly until lightly browned. Remove from the pan.
4. Add the vegetables to the pan and fry for 5 minutes, until slightly softened. Add the stock, lemon juice, and a little salt and pepper. Bring to the boil.
5. Place the chicken breasts skin side up on top of the vegetables, cover and cook gently for 30–35 minutes, until tender. Accompany with a green salad and French bread.

BRAISED DUCK

Duck breast joints include both breasts. They are a good buy as most of the meat on a duck is on the breast.

*1 duck breast joint,
   weighing 2 lb*
1 tablespoon salad oil
1 onion, chopped
2 carrots, chopped
⅔ cup white wine
*½ teaspoon grated orange
   rind*
*3 tablespoons freshly
   squeezed orange juice*

*¼ cup cream cheese,
   whipped with
   1 tablespoon lemon
   juice*
1 teaspoon cornstarch
salt and pepper to taste
*orange slices and chervil
   sprigs to garnish*

1. Trim off any excess fat from the underside of the duck breast. Heat the oil in a flameproof casserole, add the duck, skin side down, and fry until well browned. Turn

and fry the other side. Remove and drain on paper towels.
2. Add the onion and carrot to the pan and fry until slightly softened. Add the wine and stir well, scraping up any sediment from the base of the pan. Add the orange rind, juice, and salt and pepper and bring to the boil.
3. Return the duck to the pan, cover and cook gently for 45 minutes, until tender. Remove the duck and keep warm.
4. Skim the sauce, then puree in a blender or food processor and return to the pan.
5. Blend the cream cheese mixture with the cornstarch, stir into the pan and cook until thickened. Season.
6. Carefully remove the duck meat from the bone and slice thinly. Spoon a pool of sauce over each warm plate and arrange the duck on top. Garnish with halved orange slices and chervil.

Serves 4
Preparation time:
30 minutes
Cooking time:
45 minutes
Freezing:
Not recommended

FRUITED GAME CASSEROLE

Choose plump birds for this casserole. The pheasant need not be the most young and tender specimen as the long slow cooking will tenderize an older bird.

2 tablespoons salad oil
1 pheasant
2 pigeons or squab
2 onions, chopped
2 carrots, chopped
3 celery sticks, chopped
2 cups red wine
²/3 cup water

2 bay leaves
2 tablespoons softened
  butter
¹/4 cup all-purpose flour
¹/4 cup ruby port
²/3 cup raisins
salt and pepper to taste

Serves 4
Preparation time:
40 minutes
Cooking time:
1³/4–2¹/4 hours
Freezing:
Recommended

1. Heat the oil in a flameproof casserole, add the pheasant and pigeons or squab and fry until browned all over. Drain off any excess oil, then add the onion, carrot, celery, wine, water, bay leaves, and salt and pepper. Bring to the boil, then cover and simmer for 1¹/2–2 hours, until the meat is tender.

2. Lift out the birds and strip the meat from the bones. Chop into large pieces and return to the pan.

3. Place the butter and flour in a small bowl and work together with a teaspoon until well mixed. Add the paste, in small pieces, to the liquid and simmer, stirring, until thickened and smooth.

4. Add the port and raisins and simmer for 15 minutes. Check the seasoning and remove the bay leaves. Serve from the dish, accompanied by broccoli and cauliflower florets and sauteed potatoes.

TURKEY FILLETS WITH ASPARAGUS AND PERNOD SAUCE

¹/2 lb asparagus
2 teaspoons all-purpose
  flour
4 turkey fillets, each
  weighing about ¹/4 lb
2 tablespoons butter

2 shallots, chopped
1¹/4 cups Chicken Stock*
1 small potato, chopped
  finely
1 tablespoon Pernod
salt and pepper to taste

1. Remove the asparagus tips and set aside. Peel the stalks and slice thinly.

2. Season the flour with salt and pepper and use to coat the turkey fillets.

3. Heat the butter in a large frying pan with a lid. Add the turkey fillets and fry quickly on both sides until browned. Remove from the pan.

4. Add the shallots to the pan and fry until softened. Add the asparagus stalks and fry for 2 minutes. Add the stock, potato, Pernod, and salt and pepper and bring to the boil.

5. Return the turkey fillets to the pan, cover and simmer for 10–12 minutes, until the potato and asparagus are cooked and the turkey is tender.

6. Meanwhile, cook the asparagus tips in lightly salted water for 5–6 minutes, until just tender; drain.

7. Transfer the turkey fillets to warmed serving plates with a slotted spoon. Puree the sauce in a blender or food processor and pour around the turkey. Garnish with the asparagus tips and serve with a green salad.

Serves 4
Preparation time:
20 minutes
Cooking time:
About 15 minutes
Freezing:
Not recommended

HAM AND APRICOT ROLLS

⅓ cup chopped dried apricots	1 small head celeriac, cut into sticks
½ cup fresh brown breadcrumbs	⅔ cup Rich Vegetable Stock*
1 onion, chopped finely	salt and pepper to taste
1 tablespoon chopped parsley	FOR THE SAUCE:
2 tablespoons butter, melted	⅔ cup red wine
4 thin ham steaks	2 tablespoons redcurrant jelly
2 leeks, cut into strips	grated rind and juice of 1 orange and 1 lemon
	1 teaspoon Dijon mustard

Serves 4
Preparation time:
35 minutes
Cooking time:
35 minutes
Freezing:
Recommended

1. Mix together the apricots, breadcrumbs, onion, parsley and butter. Season lightly with salt and pepper.
2. Divide the mixture between the ham steaks and roll up. Secure with fine string or cocktail sticks.
3. Place the leeks and celeriac in an ovenproof dish, arrange the ham rolls on top and add the stock. Cover and cook in a 350°F oven for 35 minutes, until the ham and vegetables are tender.
4. Place all the sauce ingredients in a small pan and bring to the boil, stirring, then simmer for 5 minutes.
5. Arrange the vegetables and ham rolls on a warmed serving dish and serve with the sauce and zucchini.

VENISON AND REDCURRANT CASSEROLE

2 lb stewing venison, cut into 1 inch cubes	2 onions
2 cups red wine	½ lb sliced bacon, halved
2 cloves garlic, bruised	1 tablespoon all-purpose flour
2 strips lemon rind	⅔ cup Rich Beef Stock*
2 tablespoons lemon juice	1 cup redcurrants
3 tablespoons olive oil	¼ cup redcurrant jelly
1 cinnamon stick	salt and pepper to taste

1. Place the venison in a bowl and pour over the wine. Add the garlic, lemon rind and juice, 2 tablespoons of the oil and the cinnamon stick. Cover and leave to marinate in the refrigerator overnight.

2. Remove the venison with a slotted spoon and dry on paper towels; strain and reserve the marinade.

3. Cut each onion into 6 wedges. Stretch the bacon with the back of a knife, then roll up each piece.

4. Heat the remaining oil in a flameproof casserole, add the onion, fry until lightly browned, then remove.

5. Add the bacon rolls to the casserole and fry gently until they are lightly colored. Remove with a slotted spoon.

6. Add the venison to the pan and fry until browned all over. Sprinkle in the flour and cook for 1 minute. Gradually stir in the reserved marinade and the stock and bring to the boil. Return the onions and bacon to the pan and stir well. Season with pepper, then cover and simmer for 2 hours, until the venison is tender.

7. Add the redcurrants and jelly to the pan and simmer for 10 minutes, until the redcurrants are tender and the jelly dissolved. Taste and add salt if necessary.

8. Serve with braised fennel and baked potatoes, topped with sour cream and chives.

Serves 4–6
Preparation time:
30 minutes, plus marinating
Cooking time:
2¼ hours
Freezing:
Recommended

BASIC STOCK RECIPES

CHICKEN STOCK

2 lb chicken thighs, wings,
  drumsticks, or a mixture
  of these
1 onion
2 cloves
bouquet garni

celery leaves
2 slices fresh root ginger
10 black peppercorns
1/2 teaspoon salt
8 cups water

Makes 6–8 cups
Preparation time:
15 minutes, plus
cooling
Cooking time:
2 hours
Freezing:
Recommended

1. Cut up the chicken into small pieces and place in a large saucepan. Stick the onion with the cloves and add to the pan with the bouquet garni, celery leaves, ginger, peppercorns and salt.
2. Add the water and bring slowly to simmering point, skimming the surface with a slotted spoon. Simmer the stock very gently, uncovered, for 2 hours, skimming occasionally.
3. Strain through a fine sieve into a large bowl and leave until cold. Remove any fat from the surface. Freeze in usable amounts.

RICH VEGETABLE STOCK

This concentrated stock is ideal as a base for casseroles, or can be served as a soup just as it is. Dilute it to make a lighter stock for sauces, etc.

2 carrots, chopped
3 potatoes, chopped
2 onions, chopped
1/3 cup mushroom stalks
2 celery sticks, chopped
bouquet garni

2 bay leaves
8 black peppercorns
1 ripe tomato, chopped
8 cups water
salt to taste

Makes about
8 cups
Preparation time:
20 minutes, plus
cooling
Cooking time:
1 1/2–2 hours
Freezing:
Recommended

1. Place all the ingredients in a large saucepan and bring to the boil. Simmer very gently, uncovered, for 1 1/2–2 hours, until the vegetables are very tender.
2. Strain through a sieve into a large bowl in batches, pressing through as many of the vegetables as possible. Leave until cold, then freeze in usable amounts.

LIGHT MEAT STOCK

This is a basic stock for using up leftover bones from a joint or chicken or turkey carcass. Giblets can also be added for extra flavor.

2 lb meat bones or carcass,
   cooked or uncooked
8 cups water
2 onions, chopped
2 celery sticks, chopped

2 carrots, chopped
6 black peppercorns
bouquet garni
salt to taste

1. Place the bones or carcass in a large saucepan and cover with the water. Bring slowly to a gentle boil, skimming the surface regularly with a slotted spoon.
2. Add the remaining ingredients, partly cover and simmer for 3–4 hours, until clear.
3. Strain through a fine sieve into a large bowl and leave until cold. Remove any fat from the surface. Freeze in usable amounts.

Makes about
6 cups
Preparation time:
15 minutes, plus cooling
Cooking time:
3–4 hours
Freezing:
Recommended

RICH BEEF STOCK

Use this stock for rich beef casseroles to give depth of flavor and a good rich color.

1 lb knuckle of veal,
   chopped
1 lb shin of beef, chopped
8 cups water
1 onion, unpeeled,
   quartered

1 carrot, chopped
1 celery stick, chopped
bouquet garni
6 black peppercorns
salt to taste

1. Place the bones and beef in a large saucepan and cover with the water. Bring slowly to the boil, skimming the surface regularly with a slotted spoon. Simmer for 30 minutes.
2. Add the remaining ingredients, partly cover and simmer for 3 hours; do not allow the liquid to boil hard as this will make it cloudy.
3. Strain through a fine sieve into a large bowl and leave until cold. Remove any fat from the surface. Freeze in usable amounts.

Makes about
6 cups
Preparation time:
20 minutes, plus cooling
Cooking time:
3½ hours
Freezing:
Recommended

INDEX

Photography by: Sara Taylor
Designed by: Sue Storey
Home economist: Mary Cadogan
Stylist: Tessa Rosier
Jacket photography by: Clive Streeter
Illustration by: Linda Smith
U.S. Consultant Editor: Carla Capalbo